Mail It . . .
From Here to There

by Kim Borland

PEARSON

Scott
Foresman

Editorial Offices: Glenview, Illinois • Parsippany, New Jersey • New York, New York
Sales Offices: Needham, Massachusetts • Duluth, Georgia • Glenview, Illinois
Coppell, Texas • Ontario, California • Mesa, Arizona

Have you ever wondered how a letter gets to you? Maybe it has traveled from a nearby town. Maybe it has traveled from another state. Maybe it has traveled over the ocean from another country!

One thing is for sure. Today, mail can travel almost anywhere in the world in a short time—usually just a few days. In the past, however, mail took much longer to get from place to place.

A modern mail sorting facility

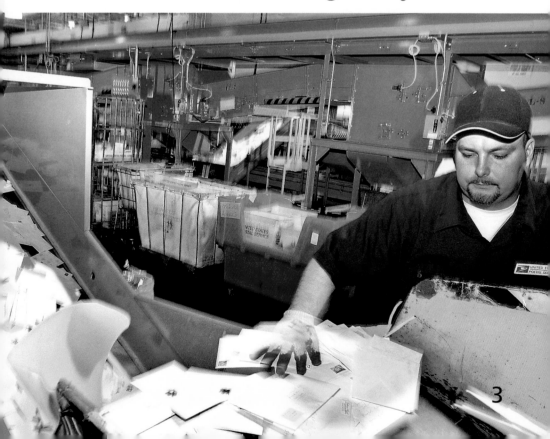

The Stagecoach

The first mail system in the United States was set up in Boston, Massachusetts, in 1639. Later on, mail was carried by stagecoach. A stagecoach is a large horse-drawn carriage.

As more and more people came to live on the East Coast of America, better roads were built and better mail routes were planned. The routes went as far west as Missouri, but there they stopped. Deserts and mountains in the West made the area dangerous to cross. Very few people traveled to the West at that time.

It took days, weeks, even months for mail to travel great distances by stagecoach.

In 1848, all this changed because of the Gold Rush. During the Gold Rush, thousands of people started traveling west to find gold. When they arrived, they wanted to **correspond** with their friends and family at home in the East.

Stagecoaches took twenty days or more to **transport** mail from Missouri to California. People wanted a faster way to send mail across the country.

Some men had the idea to start a service called the Pony Express. They hired eighty riders to carry mail on horseback between Missouri and California. They promised delivery within ten days or less. The cost of **postage** for a letter was $5.00. Pony Express service began on April 3, 1860. It was a long journey—more than 1,800 miles—and a dangerous one. Riders had to cross some of the roughest land in the country.

PONY EXPRESS

St. JOSEPH, MISSOURI to CALIFORNIA
in 10 days or less.

6

Pony Express riders rode day and night. Each rider carried the mail along a section of the long route. After seventy-five to one hundred miles of riding, the mail pouch was passed to a new rider.

The journey was difficult for the horses too. Those long trips at full speed made the horses tired. To make good time, a rider had to change horses every ten to fifteen miles.

The Pony Express advertised its ability to transport mail swiftly across the country.

PONY EXPRESS !

CHANGE OF
TIME !

NEWS!!

REDUCED
RATES !

10 Days to San Francisco!

Soon the Pony Express wasn't needed anymore. On October 24, 1861, the Pony Express made its last delivery. During the nineteen months that the Pony Express lasted, at least eighty riders and four hundred horses traveled more than 600,000 miles. That's almost as far as twenty-four trips around the world!

Meanwhile, life in the West was changing. By the late 1860s, the railroad had improved. People extended the railroad tracks much farther than before. Mail began traveling by train. People kept looking for new and even faster ways to **communicate.**

Pony Express riders are remembered on special coins.

The Telegraph

In 1832, Samuel Morse came up with the idea of using electricity to communicate. He began working on a machine that would allow him to send messages over wires. He called this new way of communicating the **telegraph.**

Samuel Morse

It took a lot of time and work to set up electrical wires across the country.

Morse created a code for sending messages. A man working with Morse helped improve the code, but it was Morse's idea, so it was called Morse code. In 1844, Morse built the first long-distance telegraph system. It was amazingly fast! Soon, people everywhere were communicating through Morse's "talking wires." The telegraph remained important for more than 100 years.

The Morse Code

In Morse code, each letter is represented by a pattern of dots and dashes. To send a telegraph message, the sender taps out the dots and dashes. The receiver reads the dots and dashes and translates them into a written message.

The telegraph was fast, but it was expensive. It was difficult to send long letters in code. The telegraph was used mainly for short, important messages.

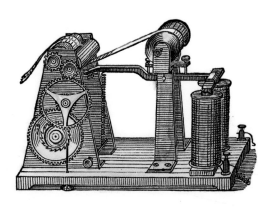

A dash in Morse code means a long tap on the machine. A dot is a short tap.

A . –	J . – – –	S . . .	2 . . – – –
B – . . .	K – . –	T –	3 . . . – –
C – . – .	L . – . .	U . . –	4 . . . . –
D – . .	M – –	V . . . –	5 . . . . .
E .	N – .	W . – –	6 – . . . .
F . . – .	O – – –	X – . . –	7 – – . . .
G – – .	P . – – .	Y – . – –	8 – – – . .
H	Q – – . –	Z – – . .	9 – – – – .
I . .	R . – .	1 . – – – –	0 – – – – –

11

The Transcontinental Railroad

Telegraphs were fast but expensive, and you couldn't use them to send a package. Packages had to be carried. During this time, steam-powered railroad trains were improving. This meant that trains carrying mail could move even faster. But trains still could not travel all the way across the country.

On May 10, 1869, that changed. Railroad tracks that connected the East with the West were completed. The **transcontinental** railroad was finished.

Soon trains could move east and west at all times of the day and night. Mail could travel across the country in about one week.

The transcontinental railroad linked the United States from east to west.

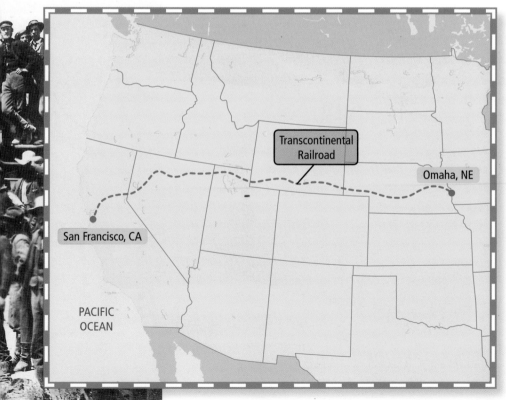

Transcontinental Railroad

Omaha, NE

San Francisco, CA

PACIFIC OCEAN

Airplanes

Airplanes were invented in the early 1900s. Just a few years later, people started using airplanes to send mail.

In 1918, an American pilot made the first mail flight in the United States. By 1920, airplanes were carrying the mail regularly. A few years later, mail could be flown right across the country.

Early mail plane

Any piece of mail, large or small, that is transported in an airplane is called airmail. Airmail is still the fastest way to send letters and packages from one place to another. Today, most mail spends at least part of its trip in an airplane.

Modern mail plane

What will be next?

New inventions continue to change the way we communicate. You probably communicate by computer. Computers can be used to send email messages to friends and family. Did you know that once a message is typed out and sent, it takes only seconds to reach another computer anywhere in the world?

Each new invention or idea has helped people communicate more easily and quickly. Next time you get a letter, think about the inventions and ideas that made it possible for you to receive it.

You can send a letter by email from your computer and only have to wait minutes for a reply.

Now Try This

Design a Postage Stamp

A postage stamp is an important part of sending a letter from one place to another. Your letter won't get very far without one!

Look at the stamp on this page. Stamps come in different designs. Some stamps celebrate important days in history. Some celebrate people. This stamp celebrates an idea you read about in this book.

Now it's your turn to design a postage stamp.

1. Brainstorm five things you could celebrate on your stamp. Maybe you'd like to show your school. Maybe you'd like to show an important day in history. Maybe you'd like to show an important day in your life.

2. Choose your favorite idea.

3. Now draw a rough draft of your design.

4. Draw your final copy on a large sheet of white construction paper.

5. Share your stamp design with your class.

ST. JOSEPH

UNITED STATES POSTAGE

4 c

Glossary

communicate *v.* to give or exchange information or news.

correspond *v.* to exchange letters with someone.

postage *n.* the amount paid for anything sent by mail.

telegraph *n.* a way of sending coded messages over wires by means of electricity.

transcontinental *adj.* describing something that crosses a continent.

transport *v.* to carry something from one place to another.